FAITH FOUNDATION

7 DAYS OF FACING FEARS AND OVERCOMING DOUBTS

RAINAH DAVIS

FAITH FOUNDATION

7 DAYS OF FACING FEARS AND OVERCOMING DOUBTS

Book Project Management by Raindrop Creative, Inc. | StartWrite Publish Team
Editorial Team: Gerald C. Simmons | Tiara Brown | Cherie Graham | Jennifer Eiland
Cover Art: Raindrop Creative Design Team

978-1-970179-90-3 Paperback
978-1-970179-91-0 eBook

This book is a part of the ***Activate Your Faith*** Devotional Series.
Activate Your Faith: The Art of Facing Fiery Trials
978-1-970179-77-4 Paperback
978-1-970179-04-0 eBook

The other two books in the series are:

Fragmented: 7 Days of Fixing Fractured Faith
978-1-970179-79-8 Paperback
978-1-970179-80-4 eBook

Future Forward Faith: 7 Days to Believe Beyond Right Now for What's Next
978-1-970179-95-8 Paperback
978-1-970179-94-1 eBook

DEDICATION

To my children – may you find faith early,
and never let it go.

To my parents – thank you for helping me find
faith early and praying for me unwaveringly
until I believed for myself.

To my husband – thank you for always having faith
in me and showing me that sometimes faith
requires a fight.

PREFACE

This devotional has been rewritten three times. The version in your hands was the one God knew you would need at this time. The original chapters have been sliced and redistributed to teach you the art of facing every trial you face in the Activate Your Faith book series. The book is divided into three sections to clarify the different aspects of faith. Each week you will have a daily devotion that ties to a theme for that timeframe:

Week 1 | Faith Foundation: 7 Days of Facing Fears and Overcoming Doubts

Week 2 | Fragmented: 7 Days of Facing Fractured Faith

Week 3 | Future Forward Faith: 7 Days to Believe Beyond right now for what's next

The devotional in your possession are the first seven days of that 21-day devotional. I was compelled to make each section their own seven-day devotional, so you do not have to wait until the entire book is available.

Now, more than likely, you are grown. Therefore, I am not telling you what to do, and I would not dare try! I have five children over the age of 18, so I know grown people will do what they want (smile). However, I recommend you block off the next 21 days and go through the days in a quiet place. Also, I encourage you to do the activities at the end of each day.

I would love for you to do a personal mini-Bible study on the Biblical encounters and historical references that stand out to you. Studying the art of anything is to approach it from a multi-faceted level. Also, the art of facing trials with fiery faith sets you up strategically and psychologically to minimize damage and the wasting of resources. This knowledge is vital because before winning a battle, you must survive it first. Since in this life, we will face struggles, the idea is to meet each challenge in boldness and strength, relying on your faith in God. This book will serve as a powerful tool in your arsenal against the fiery trials attempting to quench your faith.

AUTHOR'S NOTE

As I write the third intro to this book, I am in awe of the providence and timing of God. Six years ago this month, I was released from my job. As the days passed and months rolled in and out, it would be years before I understood why God would have allowed that event to occur.

Maybe you, like me, are staring at the face of a fiery trial in real-time. If so, then I have good news for you. There is an art to facing fiery trials. The way a pianist's fingers glide over the ivory keys or a relay runner completes a good baton handoff during track and field events is the same type of rhythm and execution needed to activate your faith.

I am in the midst of another transition as I pen these words to you. God has burdened me to complete this book in this specific season. Many of the personal stories you will read in this work are years old, but the principles

I learned and will share with you are sound. It is an honor to join arm and arm with you through the fire. I assure you that the Lord is with us, and when we come out, there will not be a hint of smoke on us. I love you, and I am cheering for you. So, let's get started!

Rainah

Contents

INTRODUCTION

I started this devotional series almost ten years ago and have added to it every few years. Still, unfortunately, other projects have taken priority over it. In November 2019, I was blessed to see Todd Galberth, my good friend, brother, create a dynamic worship experience for his live recording. Todd is also the author of the *Activate Your Faith* foreword. Listening to him share his powerful testimony and the faith that it took for him to produce this anointed and majestic experience inspired me to complete this unfinished work.

I had just released another *Activate* book designed to educate and empower individuals to develop the mindset necessary to start their businesses. During Todd>s recording, I realized that no matter what industry a person is in, it takes faith to step out and do something extraordinary with passion and guts! I was in awe as I remembered God had allowed us to remain connected for almost a decade. I met Todd at World Overcomers Christian Church, where we both worked. He was one of the church›s dynamic worship leaders. I vividly recall worshiping and crying out to God during his worship sets. In truth, his energetic, anointed, and intense praise and worship services helped me make it through one of the worst storms of my life. Therefore, it seemed fitting to have him be a part of this devotional series. Shortly after, I started working on the book but was halted again by the COVID-19 pandemic that shut down the entire world.

And here we are again; in the fall of 2022, Todd released a single to the album I mentioned above called ***He Won't Fail***. The song ministered to me profoundly, and again I was prompted to complete the entire 21-day devotional. As well as create three mini-devotionals. The one you are reading is the first in the set, I pray it encourages you. Let's get into it!

WHEN GOD SAYS NO

In 2010, I faced the most difficult trial of my life—the burial of a marriage that had figuratively died, decayed, and rotted many years earlier. I spent years praying, fasting, and begging God to revive and resurrect a relationship that was no longer beneficial for me. Thankfully, God denied my requests and pleas in an obvious and final way. Although devastated, I yielded to the undeniable "No" that I had heard from the Heavens and began to prepare myself and my daughters for a move that was unexpected for them and unknown to me.

In December 2010, I stepped out on faith and moved into a tiny house with my four daughters, ages fourteen to five. However, praise be unto God; at first, we survived, and then we thrived. Today at the time of this writing, not only am I remarried, but I am also the absolute happiest I have ever been. For years, I battled against the depression that convinced me I would lose my mind. Seriously, the enemy had me convinced that I would eventually end up having what my grandmother used to refer to as "a mental breakdown," which would leave me locked up in a padded cell and wearing a straitjacket for the rest of my life. However, as the hit gospel duo so eloquently put it: "But He didn't see fit to let none of these things be...You keep on, keeping on, keeping me..." (Artist: Mary Mary/Song: "Thank You"/2002 Incredible Album). God kept me and brought me out stronger than ever.

Now I have a testimony! The same way God kept me, He can keep you, as the old saints would say, "He'll keep you when you can't keep yourself!" God is a "keeper," and I have experienced His "keeping power," which is so astounding that I want to help you experience it, too.

During the next 21 days, my goal is to help you face whatever trials you are experiencing with fearless faith and abundant joy. The Book of James admonishes us in James 1, verses 2-4: "2 My brethren, count it all joy when you fall into various trials, 3 knowing that the testing of your faith produces patience. 4 But let patience have its perfect work, that you may be perfect and complete, lacking nothing."

Then in 1 Peter 4, verses 12-13 we read: "12 Beloved, do not think it strange concerning the fiery trial which is to try you, as though some strange thing happened to you; 13 but rejoice to the extent that you partake of Christ's sufferings, that when His glory is revealed, you may also be glad with exceeding joy."

The passage in James reveals that "the trial" actually has a purpose and that if we yield to the purpose of "this trial," we actually gain "perfection and completion." In 1 Peter, we are instructed not to be caught off guard when trials approach us because our partaking in suffering, as our Savior did, will result in our having "exceeding joy" once His glory is revealed. Hence, the Bible is clear that we should embrace trials. We should face fiery trials, knowing there is a purpose at the end of the tribulation.

Yet unfortunately, this directive is much easier said than followed. So, over the next 21 days, I want to help you develop the skill set to face your trials with fearless faith, knowing that God will bring you out of every difficulty you face. There is an art to facing trials, specifically the fiery ones that we believe were sent to take us out!

Before I give you a formula for enduring the test, I must inform you that there are different kinds of trials. The Word admonishes us that in all our *getting*, we need to endeavor to get an *understanding*. Understanding is often the difference between being able to endure something or break under the weight of the pressure produced by it.

There are three basic kinds of trials that you will face during your Christian walk:

1. **TRIAL TYPE #1**—Discipline from the Lord, based on previous sin or natural consequences based on unwise decisions.

2. **TRIAL TYPE** #2—Persecution and suffering for living a Christian life.

3. **TRIAL TYPE** #3—Attacks and temptation from demonic forces sent to distract or destroy you.

Trial Type #1

The first trial type is the easiest for a mature believer to accept. Every mature saint can recount decisions that have landed them in a devastating situation. Mature people of God who face financial difficulty because of mismanagement of money conclude that "satan didn't steal their rent money." Mature believers can admit that "they spent it on "miscellaneous" items, which are frivolous or unplanned expenses that can be hard to pinpoint at the end of the budget cycle. This type of trial is a direct result of the individual's behavior, and there are consequences as a result. For example:

If you don't pay your rent or mortgage = You will no longer have a place to stay.

If you cheat on your spouse repeatedly = You will eventually lose your spouse.

If you miss too many days from work = You will lose your job at some point.

If you get too many speeding tickets and don't drive at safe speeds = You could ultimately lose your license, car, or life.

There are also spiritual consequences for sin. The Word warns us that the wages of sin are death. We must be diligent in making better spiritual decisions, so we don't jeopardize our relationship with Christ.

Many believers repeatedly find themselves in a cycle of chastening from the Lord or reaping the consequences of destructive life "choices." It is vitally important that we master sin and make good decisions because this is the only type of trial that we have control over in our lives. The other two are based on God's permission or permissive will. Trial type is reduced or even eliminated based upon your decisions. I encourage you to stop the cycle of consequences with which you find yourself by asking the Lord to help you with your decision-making process. We will talk about this matter in more detail throughout this book.

Trial Type #2

The second type of trial we face is inevitable. John 15:18-20 (NIV) reveals: "18 If the world hates you, keep in mind that it hated Me first. 19 If you belonged to the world, it would love you as its own. As it is, you do not belong to the world, but I have chosen you out of the world. That is why the world hates you. 20 Remember what I told you: 'A servant is not greater than his master.' If they persecuted me, they will persecute you also..."

This Scripture informs us that every believer will suffer because of their faith. It isn't popular preaching; therefore, many speakers and ministers do not adequately remind us of this spiritual "fallout," but it is still the truth. A relationship with Christ doesn't give you a "trouble-free life" pass. In fact, the more havoc you wreck on the kingdom of satan you may find that the attacks against you often increase. When this counterattack occurs, you must get closer to the Lord and ensure that you don't allow the trial to push you further away. In truth, once you reach maturity and are unshakeable in your Christian walk, the enemy will often attack you or those closest to you. "The weakest links" in your life will take hits designed to impact or stop you. These types of attacks usually accompany the last kind of trial.

Trial Type #3

The third type of trial we face is the kind that makes us the most upset and is the most often assumed. When we first receive salvation, we believe that every challenge comes from our adversary, satan. However, as we mature in Christ, we learn that everything is not of the devil. Yet, because we know that even Jesus was tempted by satan, the enemy is coming for us. The Word defines satan's assignment quite specifically is to "kill, steal and destroy."

This assignment does not need any more defining and doesn't leave much to the imagination. The old saints taught us that the Bible says, "*When* your day of evil comes," and not "*If* your day of evil comes," because each of us has a day of evil that will surely come.

The Bible is also explicit on how to handle this type of trial. There are so many verses that minister to us on how to overcome temptation. We will explore some of them more in-depth throughout our seven-day journey together.

Two Keys to Overcoming Temptation

I n the following Scriptures, there are some main points I want you to meditate upon:

> 1 Corinthians 10:13 (ESV) - "No temptation has overtaken you that is not common to man. God is faithful, and He will not let you be tempted beyond your ability, but with the temptation, He will also provide the way of escape, that you may be able to endure it."

> James 4:7 (ESV) - "Submit yourselves, therefore, to God. Resist the devil, and he will flee from you."

A. God will provide a way of escape from the temptation you face. I am amazed at how often God sends ways of escape to us that we choose to ignore. I am also throwing myself under the bus. If we are honest, we have all fallen short of the glory on this one! When He sends the interruption (like a phone call or knock at the door) right before you are getting ready to give someone a "piece of your mind," you should let yourself be interrupted. Please don't ignore the call or the knocking: yield to it. Often, some of the worst experiences we have faced involve an instance where an interruption occurred when we were getting ready to fall into temptation. Still, we ignored the interference that was sent to save us. When we submit ourselves to God and resist temptation, that temptation has no choice but to flee from us.

> Ephesians 6: 10-13 (ESV) - "Finally, be strong in the Lord and in the strength of His might. Put on the whole armor of God, that you may be able to stand against the schemes of the devil. For we do not wrestle against flesh and blood, but against the rulers, against the authorities,

against the cosmic powers over this present darkness, against the spiritual forces of evil in the heavenly places. Therefore, take up the whole armor of God, that you may be able to withstand in the evil day, and having done all, to stand firm."

B. God has given us armor, so we should put it on! Decide to be strong in the Lord because you are fighting against the armies of hell. God has given us all access to armor we can put on to withstand enemy attacks. Your armor helps to protect you so that you can stand firmly, fight bravely, and win against all evil forces.

Now that you have a basic description of the types of trials we face and what God expects of us as we meet them head-on. Let's learn how to face these trials with fearless faith and then use our knowledge to help others to do the same. We will do this by learning about the different types of faith that our Biblical ancestors applied to the challenges they faced. Every kind of faith provides the art form of facing and overcoming fiery trials.

DEVOTIONAL ONE OVERVIEW: FAITH FOUNDATION

> *James 1: 2-8 (NIV): "Consider it pure joy, my brothers, whenever you face trials of many kinds because you know that the testing of your faith develops perseverance. Perseverance must finish its work so that you may be mature and complete lacking anything. But when he asks, he must believe and not doubt because he who doubts is like a wave of the sea, blown and tossed by the wind. That man should not think he will receive anything from the Lord; he is a double-minded man, unstable in all he does."*

Formulating Foundational Faith

The first thing to understand is that believing in God doesn't exempt us from trouble. To proclaim victory over trials, we must first accept that many of them are unavoidable. As mature believers, we do not face the same obstacles as new Christians because we learn and implement the Word. Applying the Word and better decision-making establishes a foundation of faith that allows us to build our lives on the firm foundation of Christ. This bedrock enables us to withstand whatever comes our way.

To attempt and build on any other foundation is unwise. Consider the parable Jesus shares in Matthew 7:24-27 (NIV): *"Therefore, everyone who hears these words of Mine and puts them into practice is like a wise man who built his house on the rock. The rain came down, the streams rose, and the winds blew and beat against that house, yet it did not fall because it had its foundation on the rock. But everyone who hears these words of Mine and does not put them into practice is like a foolish man who built his house on sand. The rain came down, the streams rose, and the winds blew and beat against that house, and it fell with a great crash."*

Here, Jesus explains the importance of both *hearing* and *practicing* the Word of God. Both hearing and doing are essential to building anything that will stand the test of time. As you dive into the first seven days of this devotional, I pray that your foundation will become stronger than ever before. If this book were a class taught on a college campus, this first section would be classified as **FIERY TRIALS 101: FOUNDATIONS OF FAITH.** This course would be a prerequisite for the ones following it, and as a believer, this is a prerequisite for life. This is the first book is a series of Fearless Faith devotionals called *Activate Your Faith*. The Activate Your Faith book contains 21-days of devotions. These seven days are week one in that series.

This section has been crafted to give you the building blocks to build your faith from scratch or fix a faulty foundation. The goal is to help you conquer your fears and eliminate your doubts. I am honored to be your professor, exhorter, and coach through the process. Let's dig in! If these seven days are a blessing to you, I encourage you to consider reading the entire series.

Day 1 Fully Functional Faith

fully functional
ful·ly| ˈfo͝olē | adverb
func·tion·al| ˈfəNG(k)SH(ə)nəl | *adjective*

working/operating correctly, completely, to the
furthest extent, or as expected in every way

> *Ezekiel 14-37:1 (CEV)*
>
> *1 Some time later, I felt the Lord›s power take
> control of me, and his Spirit carried me to a valley
> full of bones. 2 The Lord showed me all around,
> and everywhere I looked, I saw bones that were
> dried out. 3 He said, "Ezekiel, son of man, can
> these bones come back to life?" I replied, "Lord
> God, only you can answer that."*
>
> *4 He then told me to say: "Dry bones, listen to
> what the Lord is saying to you,*
>
> *5 "I, the Lord God, will put breath in you, and
> once again you will live. 6 I will wrap you with
> muscles and skin and breathe life into you. Then
> you will know that I am the Lord."*

7 I did what the Lord said, but before I finished speaking, I heard a rattling noise. The bones were coming together! 8 I saw muscles and skin cover the bones, but they had no life in them.

9 The Lord said: Ezekiel, now say to the wind, "The Lord God commands you to blow from every direction and to breathe life into these dead bodies, so they can live again."

10 As soon as I said this, the wind blew among the bodies, and they came back to life! They all stood up, and there were enough to make a large army.

11 The Lord said: Ezekiel, the people of Israel are like dead bones. They complain that they are dried up and that they have no hope for the future. 12 So tell them, "I, the Lord God, promise to open your graves and set you free. I will bring you back to Israel, 13, and when that happens, you will realize that I am the Lord. 14 My Spirit will give you breath, and you will live again. I will bring you home, and you will know that I have kept my promise. I, the Lord, have spoken."

Everything starts with what you say. God asked the Old Testament prophet, Ezekiel, a question. He asked Ezekiel could a valley of dry bones come back to life. First, Ezekiel was not sure. He tossed the question back to God, saying, "Lord, God, only you can answer that."

The key to facing any situation is being honest about the reality of the predicament. Ezekiel was sitting in a valley of dry, dusty bones. Think about it; he was surrounded by death. There was no life, nothing moving, and no signs that life was even possible. However, God gives Ezekiel a powerful lesson we can implement for the dead situations we face. If God breathes life into it, then it can, in fact, live.

I once read that Bishop TD Jakes said that one of the most important letters he ever wrote to himself contained the sentence, "Don't die." I remember reading this text in my *Woman Thou Art Loosed Bible* that I bought in July 2000. Twenty-two years later, I just watched Bishop Jakes retire the Woman Thou Art Loosed brand (called Finally Loosed) and pass the baton to his daughter, Sarah Jakes Roberts. She will continue the movement under the name Woman Evolve. I do not want to think what would have happened if Bishop Jakes had not written that letter to himself. It is scary to think what would have happened to all the people whose lives have been touched by his ministry. I have listened to him tell stories about people still mad at him for leaving West Virginia and moving to Dallas, Texas. Even amid his accomplishments, some people are angry at his faith and obedience to God. That mindset should be a lesson to you and me that some people may never understand or agree with our faith-inspired decisions. We must believe anyway, and we must be determined to move despite the opinions of others.

Most importantly, we must be prepared to be alone. There is no mention of anyone else being in the valley when God started speaking to Ezekiel. The two of them were surrounded by lifeless, scattered bones.

Let's break down the story so we can apply it to our fiery trials.

1. God is with you.

First, Ezekiel is alone with God. This fact is worth noting because God is with you no matter what you face.

2. Speak life over the situations that you face.

Next, God tells Ezekiel what to say. We can find countless scriptures in the Bible that we can quote to stir and activate our faith. Here are a few of my favorites. I recommend you commit to memory and declare over yourself.

> *I remain confident of this: I will see the goodness of the Lord in the land of the living. (Psalm 27:13 NIV)*

> *I shall not die but live to tell of all his deeds. (Psalm 118:17 TLB)*

> *No weapon that has been made to be used against you will succeed. You will have an answer for anyone who accuses you. This is the inheritance of the Lord>s servants. Their victory comes from me," declares the Lord. (Isaiah 54:17 GW)*

> *Cast all your anxiety on him because he cares for you. (I Peter 5:7 NIV)*
>
> *For I know the plans I have for you," declares the Lord, "plans to prosper you and not to harm you, plans to give you hope and a future. (Jeremiah 29:11 NIV)*

3. Godly instructions produce miraculous results.

Before Ezekiel could finish speaking life over the bones, they began to rattle and come together. The prophet watched as the muscles and skin tissue instantly covered the bones! God then instructed the prophet to command the wind to blow in every direction to give the bones life. Not only did the bones come back to life, but there were also enough to form a large army. God provided this illustration for the children of Israel so they would know that He keeps His promises. As a result of this fulfillment, Ezekiel and the people of Israel experienced a fully functional faith. This type is a faith that understands that God never leaves us; His commands produce miracles, and He can cause dead situations to live.

God desires that your faith be fully functional. He does not want you to merely believe that He is with you but not believe that He can give you a miracle. Your Heavenly Father also doesn't want you to expect a miracle but not be willing to follow His commands. He wants your faith to function at full capacity.

Fearless Faith To-Do List: Day 1

1. Compile your favorite quotes and scriptures. List 10 here:

    1. _____

    2. _____

    3. _____

    4. _____

    5. _____

    6. _____

    7. _____

    8. _____

    9. _____

    10. _____

2. Take these quotes and scriptures and turn them into a declaration for you to say when you are facing a trial so that you can develop fully functional faith.

_____

_____

_____

_____

_____

_____

_____

_____

_____

_____

_____

_____

If you need more space, continue writing it on a separate sheet of paper.

3.) Take your declaration and put it somewhere you can see it daily. A few options for you are:

- ❖ Your bathroom
- ❖ A frame on your nightstand
- ❖ Place in your Bible
- ❖ Put up at your office.

It just needs to be somewhere you will see it and say it daily.

Day 2 Friendship Faith

friend·ship
'fren(d),SHip | *noun*

the emotions or conduct of friends • a state of
mutual trust and support between allies

> *Luke 5:17-26 (CEB)*
>
> *17 One day, when Jesus was teaching, Pharisees
> and legal experts were sitting nearby. They had
> come from every village in Galilee and Judea and
> from Jerusalem. Now the power of the Lord was
> with Jesus to heal. 18 Some men were bringing a
> man who was paralyzed, lying on a cot. They
> wanted to carry him in and place him before Jesus,
> 19, but they couldn't reach him because of the
> crowd. So, they took him up on the roof and lowered
> him—cot and all—through the roof tiles into the
> crowded room in front of Jesus. 20 When Jesus
> saw their faith, he said, "Friend, your sins are
> forgiven."*

21 The legal experts and Pharisees began to mutter among themselves, "Who is this who insults God? Only God can forgive sins!"

22 Jesus recognized what they were discussing and responded, "Why do you fill your minds with these questions? 23 Which is easier—to say, 'Your sins are forgiven,' or to say, 'Get up and walk'? 24 But so that you will know that the Human One has authority on the earth to forgive sins" —Jesus now spoke to the man who was paralyzed, "I say to you, get up, take your cot, and go home." 25 Right away, the man stood before them, picked up his cot, and went home, praising God.

26 All the people were beside themselves with wonder. Filled with awe, they glorified God, saying, "We've seen unimaginable things today."

When I conduct workshops for small businesses and churches, one of the topics I talk about in almost every session is the power of the "Intentional Inner Circle." Your IIC (as we will call it) is your personal faith crew.

You believe in them, and they believe in you. More importantly, they have a real relationship with God. Your family you love, friends you love, and co-workers you work well with--all of those people cannot be in your inner circle.

I make this statement because when facing an intense, fiery trial that has driven you close to despair, there are certain kinds of people you need to walk with you. The Bible describes them in this manner in Leviticus 26:7-8 *(NIV)*:

> *7 You will pursue your enemies, and they will fall by the sword before you. 8 Five of you will chase a hundred, and a hundred of you will chase ten thousand, and your enemies will fall by the sword before you.*

Now that is a no-joke crew! However, most of our inner circles end up being much smaller than that in the Leviticus scripture passage. My grandmother used to tell me that the number of "best friends" would continue to dwindle as I got older, and she was correct.

As every year passes, I learn to discern who I can depend on and how to categorize everyone else joyfully. As a Christian, you can love people wholeheartedly and yet not allow everyone the same level of access. My dad calls it "feeding someone out of a long-handled spoon." One of the reasons that this "grouping" is so important is when we are incapable of categorizing people correctly, the Lord often intervenes and creates situations to help us do so. I can give you an example from my own life, but first, let's unpack the passage from Luke 5 above.

Can you imagine having people in your life who care about you so much they decide that they are determined to make sure you get to the altar to be healed by Jesus? Seriously, let's unpack it. Let's imagine a group of guys are in the local barbershop getting their hair and beards trimmed when they hear that Jesus is in town for revival at the local church.

The guys remember they have a friend who is home paralyzed because back in the day, he was running the streets and received an injury that left him permanently incapacitated. Maybe it was a stray bullet, perhaps it was gang activity, maybe he was just in the wrong place at the wrong time, but it left him immobilized. So, the guys decide that they are going to see their friend and tell him about the revival. I imagine they get to the house and tell their boy about this prophet named Jesus in revival down the street. All excited, they ran down all the miracles they had already heard from others. It is possible that their homeboy expressed doubt but finally gave in and decided to go with them. (Now, remember that this story occurs during biblical times.)

Meanwhile, they get to the revival, and the crowd covers the entryway. The place is so packed the doors are inaccessible. If this were happening in the present day, it would be the equivalent of the balcony section being filled to capacity. Additionally, the overflow seating sections would also be swarming with people.

In modern-day times, the fire marshall may even be on the premises sending people away. However, in their day, the roof was not structured like buildings today. Depending on the translation you read, tiles covered the roof. In one translation, it says the men removed the tiles; in the version above, it just says they lowered him in and got him in front of Jesus. We will break down what makes this story so incredible in a minute. First, let's pause and hone in on the fact that Jesus heals the paralyzed man because of the faith of the people who brought him. Verse 20 reads:

> *"When Jesus saw **their** faith, he said, "Friend, your sins are forgiven."*

This verse blew me away when I reread this story as an adult. It was a super cool, extraordinary Sunday school story to me as a child. But, as a mature believer, it ministered to me regarding how critical the faith of the people in my inner circle is. I realized that everyone needs a faith crew in this life, so if one person's faith is weak, the other believers' faith can kick into gear!

Friendship faith does a few things:

1. **Friends with faith will literally or figuratively get you to Jesus.** In modern times, they may pick you up and take you to a Worship Night or a Sunday service. They may send you a YouTube link to a faith teacher, preacher, or leader. They also may send you an inspirational social media post or a link for a life-

changing book on Audible or Amazon by any means necessary. Friendship faith actively gets their loved ones to experience God in an intimate and meaningful way.

2. **Faith friends do not accept "no" for an answer.** Your faith crew helps you secure a second diagnosis. Friendship faith enables you to find the best doctors and applies faith while believing for your healing to manifest.

3. **Friendship faith is a faith that believes with you and even for you while waiting for your faith to catch up**. Verse 20 is proof of this assertion; Jesus was moved by the faith of the infirmed man's friends.

It is crucial that your family also have this type of faith when you are believing God for something. In December 2021, I received a disturbing phone call. My beloved, Amirah Garcia, who plays for the Howard University Women's Basketball team, had injured her leg. She had tests done, but it would be a couple of days before we had the results. When the results came back, she had torn her ACL and MCL and damaged her meniscus. We were all devastated. But, being a woman of faith, I knew we needed to apply "faith and works" to the situation.

I sprang into action. I called my husband and told him about the predicament. As a former athlete who had suffered a significant injury in high school, he was familiar with the process. He reached out to a classmate of his who was a retired orthopedic surgeon. She gave us a surgeon's name, considered the region's best. I will never forget; I researched the physician, and sure enough, her credentials matched her reputation.

Adding insult to injury, all of this unfolded one week before Christmas. I called the Duke Orthopedics' scheduling center and talked to a wonderful lady named Mary. Although she was friendly, she was a little skeptical about the odds of getting the surgeon I was calling about or any surgeon before February. The doctors' schedules were scattered because of the holiday.

Additionally, their surgical calendars were jammed because they were still rescheduling patients due to COVID-19. I told Mary we needed a Christmas miracle, and she said, "Okay," we will keep going until we get to a surgeon who can see her. I stopped her and told her we needed the best surgeon that could see her the soonest. Then she changed her approach, and we landed on the surgeon who would treat my baby. The surgeon was available for pre-op screening in three days, which meant that Amirah could have surgery during the first week of January. I learned an important lesson. During that time, I did not have time to fall apart and have a pity party. I had to cast my cares on Jesus. Focus, take control of the situation, pray to God for the best surgeon for Amirah, and get Mary to join me in my faith destination for my daughter.

I would not let Mary go until she helped me get what I needed for my baby. To this day, Amirah is healing well. She has started doing light workouts with her team, and I pray I will see her play during the 2022-2023 school year in Jesus' name.

Amirah's healing was orchestrated by God and was set in motion by her praying mother and an excellent patient services representative at Duke Hospital. God will show up as Jehovah Rophe *-our Healer/Jehovah* *heals.* We must keep the right friends and family believing with us, especially when we are too distraught or discouraged to believe for ourselves.

I want to encourage some mothers or fathers who are bombarding Heaven for healing for a child right now. God is no respecter of persons. If He can do it for us, He can do it for you. Amirah's situation is not our family's only encounter with Rophe; it is just the most recent. God has healed my mother, father, and youngest grandson, and if you want to include COVID, He has healed almost all of us from that moment! God is a healer. It is crucial, critical, and key that you get the right friends and family to believe with you. He can turn those situations around. We have to trust Him and be mindful of the company that we keep!

Fearless Faith To-Do List: Day 2

It is time to assemble your Faith Crew to activate *Friendship/Family* Faith.

List the names of everyone in your life who encourages you, ignites your faith, and generally helps you to see the positive in every situation.

_____

_____

_____

_____

_____

_____

_____

_____

_____

_____

_____

_____

Now, take the group above and list everyone in this group who has a genuine relationship with God (they live right, and you know that they pray **for real**).

_____

_____

_____

_____

_____

_____

Now, take those people who you would trust with your life, and list them:

_____

_____

_____

_____

_____

_____

These are the people you should have in your Faith Crew. The more severe the circumstances, the smaller the group must be. Everyone's faith is not set up the same. A person who can believe in you finding the right job may not be able to apply faith that you can conceive a child if you have infertility issues. Additionally, some people can believe in the Lord to heal your body if you are sick. However, that same person can't imagine the Lord releasing a family member from prison if they are locked up and serving a life sentence.

Remember that the more intense the situation, the more intentional you must become about who you have "in the room with you!" Also, remember that the faith of the paralyzed man's friends stirred God to move on the man's behalf. Make sure you have the right people for every battle you face.

Day 3 Formulated Faith

for·mu·late |
ˈfôrmyəˌlāt | verb

create or devise methodically (a strategy or a proposal): *formulate economic policy* • express (an idea) concisely or systematically

> *1 Samuel 17: 38- 40 (NCV)*
>
> *38 Saul put his own clothes on David. He put a bronze helmet on his head and dressed him in armor. 39 David put on Saul's sword and tried to walk around, but he was not used to all the armor Saul had put on him. He said to Saul, "I can't go in this because I'm not used to it." Then David took it all off. 40 He took his stick in his hand and chose five smooth stones from a stream. He put them in his shepherd's bag and grabbed his sling. Then he went to meet the Philistine.*

I have four biological children and two children by marriage. My four biological children are all girls. One of the fascinating things I have discovered about my daughters is that even though they love my sense of fashion to a point. They all love how I assemble my outfits, but two of my girls rarely like anything I pick out for them. They generally give me the same answer: "That would look great on you!"

One of the reasons for this difference is that even though they are my children, they are individuals, and each has her own unique style. In the same way, when you are facing a giant, you cannot fight it the same way everyone else does. You should fight with your own personal weapons and armor. It is critical that you formulate (methodically, strategically, and concisely plan) how to apply your faith to that challenge you face.

It would help if you chose the weapons that work for you. As I write this chapter, I have just received bad news about a family member. Not only will I be praying for that person, but I will also be praising God for their complete healing. In the past, God has met me in the midst of my praises. As a former liturgical dancer, I understand the significance of praise.

Moreover, I learned at an early age that praise is a weapon. I will share more testimonies of this throughout the faith series. For now, let's unpack David's chosen weapons.

David objected when Saul challenged David and told him that he was too inexperienced to fight against the giant warrior. In earlier verses, David informed Saul that he (David) had killed both a lion and a bear when the animals threatened the lives of his father's sheep.

We often overlook the everyday tasks that prepare us for our future destiny moments. Sometimes the most mundane, routine activities equip us for future success.

Think about it, David did not know he was preparing to face a giant when he was protecting the sheep. But imagine if he had chosen not to defend the helpless animals; David would not have been prepared for his warfare against the giant.

David's story teaches a few valuable lessons.

1. **God has already sent some "practice" trials that taught you how to fight and have prepared you to snatch victory from your enemy's clutches.** You are more powerful than you realize and know more than you realize.

As you formulate your plan of attack, I encourage you to reflect on your life; what has God already brought you through? What troubles have you overcome that another person may not have survived? Whatever those situations are, please know that you acquired some weapons because of those battles. You can now access that artillery to help you face today's giants. The incredible thing about your weapons is that they fit you, and you know exactly how to use them. That is why David had to refuse the armor of the king.

David couldn't carry Saul's sword because he was not used to fighting with it. David had to use a weapon that he was already skilled at using. He picked up five of these weapons and prepared to face the giant with the sling in his bag, the same weapon he used to save the lives of the sheep.

2. **When facing your giant (trial), you must go into that battle with a weapon you are familiar with using.** It is crucial to fight with equipment that can help you win because many of our weapons for the next battle are gained in the warfare that preceded it.

For this reason, it is crucial to refrain from punking out prematurely. You may wonder, how do I do that? "How do I find the faith to fight the lions and bears so I am prepared when I face Goliath?" Whew, I am so glad that you asked.

The first answer is:

1. You must have a prayer life and learn to trust God.

The old folks would say, "You better know the Lord for yourself!" You cannot face a Goliath-sized trial on the backs of other people's prayers. Your parents may pray for you, but that is not enough when you are facing a test that seems larger than life. David's weapon was a slingshot and five stones. Notice that David had to have all of it to fight effectively; he needed his weapon in his hand and faith in his heart. He trusted God to deliver him because God had been with him before.

You must seek God in praise and worship. We learn that David was a worshiper. He danced before the Lord so vibrantly in his later life that his wife was ashamed

59

of him. Also, he was such a skilled harpist that the evil spirits tormenting King Saul fled when David played for him.

1. You have to be faithful over the few, so God can make you ruler over many. *(Scripture Reference: Matthew 25:23 KJV)*

Again, had David not felt that the sheep were important enough to protect, he would not have had the experience needed to execute his faith against the giant. A life intertwined with prayer, praise and worship is an effective composite of weapons when you are waging war against the enemy. Trying to engage in warfare with only one of these things is ineffectively having the slingshot without the stones or (in modern-day times) a gun without bullets.

Something happens to you when you develop a lifestyle of prayer, praise, and worship. You ignite a close, intimate relationship with God. You can hear His voice more clearly and quickly. Indeed, you are not so easily distracted by the world's noise. In addition, you are not bothered by the attacks of the enemy because you recognize them as the attacks they are—no more and no less. You also trust God more because you sin less when you pray regularly and worship Him. It is similar to working out; when I am on track with my workout routine, I do not crave the same types of food when I miss the gym.

In the same way, when you fellowship God regularly, your flesh is subject to your spirit. In other words, your "flesh" (your soul) does not rule you. Of course, none of us is without sin, but the more righteous we are, the more we trust Him because we know we have not done anything to block His blessings or deliverance.

There is one last principle I want to add to assist you with formulating your faith; however, it may be the most critical.

Expect to win but be prepared to miss.

David picked up five stones, not one. We must be prepared for long battles. There are things that God will move on instantly. We all love when God shows up suddenly in scripture. We love the "about midnight" miracles. However, we need stamina if the breakthrough takes some time. Many people are strong enough to weep through the night, but what happens when their joy doesn't come the next morning?

A key ingredient to developing stamina is the discipline to do the things you do not want to do. It stands to reason that David was sick of the sheep, especially after the prophet anointed David king, but he continued to do his job. The ordinary, monotonous, mundane task of sheep herding prepared David for his most epic contest. We, too, must develop the discipline to be prepared to formulate our faith for both quick wins and hard-fought victories.

Fearless Faith To-Do List: Day 3

List your faith weapons and how you acquired them.

_____

_____

_____

_____

_____

_____

_____

_____

_____

_____

_____

_____

_____

Think of the battle(s) you are currently facing and what you need your weapons specifically for those trials. List them below.

_____

_____

_____

_____

_____

_____

Record the date, day, and year when God shows up and grants you victory. Also, document how you strategically used your weapons.

_____

_____

_____

_____

_____

_____

Day 4 Fast-Action Faith

fast - ac·tion |
fast - ˈakSHən | adjective

the process of doing something, typically to
achieve an aim at high speed: within a short
time: taking effect quickly

1 Sam 25:2; 4-35 (NIV)

*2 A certain man in Maon, who had property there
at Carmel, was very wealthy. He had a thousand
goats and three thousand sheep, which he was
shearing in Carmel. 3 His name was Nabal, and
his wife's name was Abigail. She was an intelligent
and beautiful woman, but her husband was surly
and mean in his dealings—he was a Calebite.*

*4 While David was in the wilderness, he heard
that Nabal was shearing sheep. 5 So he sent ten
young men and said to them, "Go up to Nabal at
Carmel and greet him in my name. 6 Say to him:
'Long life to you! Good health to you and your
household! And good health to all that is yours!*

7 *"Now I hear that it is sheep-shearing time. When your shepherds were with us, we did not mistreat them, and the whole time they were at Carmel, nothing of theirs was missing. 8 Ask your own servants, and they will tell you. Therefore be favorable toward my men since we come at a festive time. Please give your servants and your son David whatever you can find for them."'*

9 When David's men arrived, they gave Nabal this message in David's name. Then they waited.

10 Nabal answered David's servants, "Who is this David? Who is this son of Jesse? Many servants are breaking away from their masters these days. 11 Why should I take my bread and water, and the meat I have slaughtered for my shearers, and give it to men coming from who knows where?"

12 David's men turned around and went back. When they arrived, they reported every word. 13 David said to his men, "Each of you strap on your sword!" So they did, and David strapped his on as well. About four hundred men went up with

David, while two hundred stayed with the supplies.

14 One of the servants told Abigail, Nabal's wife, "David sent messengers from the wilderness to give our master his greetings, but he hurled insults at them. 15 Yet these men were very good to us. They did not mistreat us, and the whole time we were out in the fields near them, nothing was missing. 16 Night and day, they were a wall around us the whole time we were herding our sheep near them. 17 Now think it over and see what you can do because disaster is hanging over our master and his whole household. He is such a wicked man that no one can talk to him."

18 Abigail acted quickly. She took two hundred loaves of bread, two skins of wine, five dressed sheep, five seahs of roasted grain, a hundred cakes of raisins, and two hundred cakes of pressed figs and loaded them on donkeys. 19 Then she told her servants, "Go on ahead; I'll follow you." But she did not tell her husband, Nabal.

20 As she came riding her donkey into a mountain ravine, there were David and his men descending toward her, and she met them. 21 David had just said, "It's been useless—all my watching over this fellow's property in the wilderness so that nothing of his was missing. He has paid me back evil for good. 22 May God deal with David, be it ever so severely if by morning I leave alive one male of all who belong to him!"

23 When Abigail saw David, she quickly got off her donkey and bowed down before David with her face to the ground. 24 She fell at his feet and said: "Pardon your servant, my lord, and let me speak to you; hear what your servant has to say. 25 Please pay no attention, my lord, to that wicked man Nabal. He is just like his name—his name means Fool, and folly goes with him. And as for me, your servant, I did not see the men my lord sent. 26 And now, my lord, as surely as the Lord your God lives and as you live, since the Lord has kept you from bloodshed and from avenging yourself with your own hands, may your enemies and all who are intent on harming my lord be like Nabal. 27 And let this gift, which your servant has brought to my lord, be given to the men who follow you.

28 "Please forgive your servant's presumption. The Lord, your God, will certainly make a lasting dynasty for my lord because you fight the Lord's battles, and no wrongdoing will be found in you as long as you live. 29 Even though someone is pursuing you to take your life, the life of my lord will be bound securely in the bundle of the living by the Lord your God, but the lives of your enemies he will hurl away as from the pocket of a sling. 30 When the Lord has fulfilled for my lord every good thing he promised concerning him and has appointed him ruler over Israel, 31 my lord will not have on his conscience the staggering burden of needless bloodshed or of having avenged himself. And when the Lord your God has brought my lord success, remember your servant."

32 David said to Abigail, "Praise be to the Lord, the God of Israel, who has sent you today to meet me. 33 May you be blessed for your good judgment and for keeping me from bloodshed this day and from avenging myself with my own hands. 34 Otherwise, as surely as the Lord, the God of Israel, lives, who has kept me from harming you, if *you had not come quickly to meet me, not one male belonging to Nabal would have been left alive by daybreak.*"

> *35 Then David accepted from her hand what she had brought him and said, "Go home in peace. I have heard your words and granted your request."*

Please forgive the length of the scripture; this story is not as well-known as it should be. If "faith without works" was a Bible personality, Abigail would be it. King David and his men have been watching over Nabal's land while they were out in the wilderness. David sent one of his men to inform Nabal that they had been protecting his property and requested some bread and water in return. Nabal who is drunk and name literally means "foolish", basically responds with obscenities and tells his servants to ask David to buzz off. If you know anything about David, that was the wrong way to respond to him. Well, David plans to kill every male in Nabal's household because of the insult. Nabal's wife, Abigail, hears about the pending danger heading their way and acts quickly. Verse 18 says: *"she took two hundred loaves of bread, two skins of wine, five dressed sheep, five seahs of roasted grain, a hundred cakes of raisins and two hundred cakes of pressed fig"* and sent it to David and his men. The bounty arrived before Abigail. As soon as she saw David, she quickly bowed down and begged for forgiveness on behalf of her husband to save her household. David received her kind gesture and thanked her for keeping him from unnecessary bloodshed.

Keys for Activating Fast-Acting Faith

We can learn three things from Abigail's fast-acting faith:

#1 – Faith without works is dead. Abigail did not drop down and pray that God would save them. Instead, she got to work and created a solution to the problem at hand.

#2 – She implemented her plan but did not tell the person who created the problem. We often try to solicit help from the people who are causing the challenge. We must use faith and wisdom to know the appropriate time to bring different people into the plan.

#3- She took a risk. Abigail had no proof that her solution would work; however, she got busy implementing a solution! David could have killed her on the spot, but she had faith and took a chance to change the outcome already in motion.

I am not sure if you have ever been afraid to act, but if you have, I want you to study this story from beginning to end. Abigail knew who she was married to; in a time of arranged marriages, Nabal probably was not her choice.

I recently had the opportunity to see the incredible movie *The Woman King* starring Viola Davis. Her co-star chose weapons over a wedding dress! She opted to fight in the army rather than be matched up with an older man in an arranged marriage. So, if the movie reflects Abigail›s situation, her relationship was not pleasant, and she had probably seen Nabal handle many transactions poorly. This time Abigail not only saved her household but ended up saving herself. Again, I encourage you to read chapter 25 in its entirety. It will be a blessing to you as you pray for courage to respond quickly, boldly, and wisely in every situation that requires fast-acting faith.

Fearless Faith To-Do List: Day 4

Describe a situation you are facing where you have been afraid to act.

_____

_____

_____

_____

_____

_____

_____

_____

_____

_____

_____

_____

_____

_____

Review the entire chapter of I Samuel 25. What lessons from Abigail's story can you apply to your present trial?

_____

_____

_____

_____

_____

_____

_____

_____

_____

_____

_____

_____

_____

_____

Day 5 Finally Faith

fi·nal·ly |
ˈfīn(ə)lē | adverb

after a long time, typically involving difficulty or delay • as the last in a series of related events or objects • [sentence adverb] used to introduce a final point or reason: finally, it is common knowledge that travel broadens the horizons. • in such a way as to put an end to doubt and dispute.

GENESIS 29:16-35 (NIV)

16 Now Laban had two daughters; the name of the older was Leah, and the name of the younger was Rachel. 17 Leah had weak eyes, but Rachel had a lovely figure and was beautiful. 18 Jacob was in love with Rachel and said, "I'll work for you seven years in return for your younger daughter Rachel."

19 Laban said, "It's better that I give her to you than to some other man. Stay here with me." 20 So

Jacob served seven years to get Rachel, but they seemed like only a few days to him because of his love for her.

21 Then Jacob said to Laban, "Give me my wife. My time is completed, and I want to make love to her."

22 So Laban brought together all the people of the place and gave a feast. 23 But when evening came, he took his daughter Leah and brought her to Jacob, and Jacob made love to her. 24 And Laban gave his servant Zilpah to his daughter as her attendant.

25 When morning came, there was Leah! So, Jacob said to Laban, "What is this you have done to me? I served you for Rachel, didn't I? Why have you deceived me?"

26 Laban replied, "It is not our custom here to give the younger daughter in marriage before the older one. 27 Finish this daughter's bridal week; then we will give you the younger one also, in return for another seven years of work."

28 And Jacob did so. He finished the week with Leah, and then Laban gave him his daughter Rachel to be his wife. 29 Laban gave his servant Bilhah to his daughter Rachel as her attendant. 30 Jacob made love to Rachel also, and his love for Rachel was greater than his love for Leah. And he worked for Laban another seven years.

31 When the Lord saw that Leah was not loved, he enabled her to conceive, but Rachel remained childless. 32 Leah became pregnant and gave birth to a son. She named him Reuben, for she said, "It is because the Lord has seen my misery. Surely my husband will love me now."

33 She conceived again, and when she gave birth to a son, she said, "Because the Lord heard that I am not loved, he gave me this one too." So she named him Simeon.

34 Again, she conceived, and when she gave birth to a son, she said, "Now, at last, my husband will become attached to me because I have borne him three sons." So he was named Levi.

35 She conceived again, and when she gave birth to a son, she said, "This time, I will praise the Lord." So, she named him Judah. Then she stopped having children.

This story has a personal meaning for me. When I was nineteen, I gave birth to my first daughter my freshman year of college. I got married and divorced within a two-year time span. I will share more about that at another time.

Five years later, I got pregnant and married again because, unfortunately, I did not learn my lesson the first time. This time I was determined to make the marriage work, regardless of how ill-matched the union proved to be over and over again. The arguments worsened, but I continued to "believe" that I could pray away all the dysfunction, incompatibility, and toxicity. I attempted to make my husband happy, to no avail, because in reality, he did not love me, and no matter what I did, I could not change that. Like Leah, I found myself having babies I loved so much that I was convinced their father would love them enough to want to be with us. Well, a couple of things were faulty in my immature twenty-something mind.

First and foremost, you can't make another person love you. Especially when the way you came together in the first place was questionable at best. Side note: Summer flings typically do not result in lasting, happy unions.

Next, having children will not save a marriage. In my case, we had girls, and my spouse wanted a son, and science was against him. To make matters worse, I felt as if I was being blamed for the gender of the babies since I was the vessel that the children came through.

Sometimes women think kids will make a troubled marriage better, but having more children makes a bad situation even harder to leave. If your relationship is in trouble and you have one child, it is easier to pack the two of you up than if you have three or more. I know this too well because I stayed in a relationship where I was miserable for a long time as I weighed leaving my husband and becoming a single mother of four girls. Yet, eventually, I became strong enough to pull the plug.

One day after weeping and worshiping through all three of the services we had on Sunday morning, I began to gain strength because our pastor preached a two-part series on divorce that he had never preached before. Interestingly enough, I don't know if he has ever preached again. He gave the most practical reasons for separation and divorce I had ever heard. I began to think that maybe my husband and I were just stuck, even though we most likely did not feel stuck for the same reasons. I was a mom with two different "baby daddies." Even though I was married to both of the dads, the thought still made me feel ashamed. It wasn't until I talked with my dad one day that I started on the road to my breakthrough. I told him about our pastor's sermon, and he quickly shared several things. As a matter of fact, it seemed as though he had been waiting for this moment. I will never forget the words he said to me:

"Honey, I raised you to be Rachel. You should never allow anyone to treat you and your children like Leah--second-class citizens."

Whew! As Dr. Dharius Daniels would say, "Let's pause for the cause." We need to take a moment and thank God for good dads, mentors, and role models. My dad was not throwing shade at Leah; he was letting me know that Rachel's favor and love were what he desired and planned for my life. If you go back to our text in Genesis, you will see that Jacob loved Rachel so much that he worked seven years for her hand in marriage. However, her dad Laban was so treacherous he tricked Jacob after those seven years and gave him Leah. You would think that Jacob would have walked away, but no. He worked another seven years to make Rachel his bride. My dad was ultimately saying, "Not only do I want a man to love you the way Jacob loved Rachel," but he also wanted a man that would sacrifice to that same degree. And I can happily report that "the third time is a charm" for me. Because, other than my parents and ancestors, no one has sacrificed more for my children and me than my husband, Jason Davis. Our relationship is proof for every woman or man reading this that "delayed is not denied." If you are in a relationship where you feel as if "you are an afterthought," I want you to keep believing. Or if you are "still waiting" for God's best for you, do not give up. It is time for you to develop "finally faith."

Leah was so desperate for Jacob's love that she would barter with her sister so Jacob would visit her tent at night. Leah thought bringing Jacob's seed (especially his sons) into the Earth would gain her favor with her husband. She did this three times, but on the fourth time around, she received a faith adjustment, declaring, "This time," I will praise the Lord and named her baby Judah. Then she stopped having children for a while.

I want to let you know that if you are going to have "finally" faith, you must make up your mind that God knows best. If you want a relationship, job, or possession, and you keep hitting a figurative brick wall, you will have to give that thing to the Lord. You are going to have to release that desire to Him. Leah was never loved more than Rachel, but Rachel died in childbirth, giving birth to Benjamin. Rachel had favor with Jacob, but Leah had favor with God. Sometimes, God will have you outlive, outstay, and outproduce the people that others think are better than you. The key is that you must turn it over to God. I would have never gotten a new man and a new last name had I never released the last one. Sometimes, God is waiting for us to finally release the desire, the yearning, and the need to Him. The Word teaches us in *Psalm 84:11 NIV:*

> *"For the Lord God is a sun and shield; the Lord bestows favor and honor;*
>
> *no good thing does he withhold from those whose walk is blameless."*

This verse has blessed my life ever since I heard it. It is a reminder that if I believe God for something, my belief is a "good thing," and either He is going to give it to me, and it just has not manifested yet, or I need to walk a little more blamelessly. Either way, because God's promises are yes and AMEN, I know that as long as I keep His laws and commandments, His promise is on the way. I just have to adopt a "finally faith" attitude and release it all to Him.

Fearless Faith To-Do List: Day 5

1. List one area where you need to exercise "finally faith" and release a specific burden to the Lord.

2. Find a scripture in the Word that you can insert in your prayers for the remaining 16 days of your devotional study (you can also meditate on Psalm 84:11 along with your chosen scripture.

3. Record the date that you experience the complete peace of God regarding this situation:

_____

_____

_____

_____

_____

_____

_____

_____

Day 6 Fierce Faith

fierce |
firs | adjective

having or displaying an intense or ferocious
aggressiveness

Day 6 Scripture Part 1: *2 Kings 4:8-17 (NIV)*

*8 One day, Elisha went on to Shunem, where a
wealthy woman lived, who urged him to eat some
food. So, whenever he passed that way, he would
turn in there to eat food. 9 And she said to her
husband, "Behold now, I know that this is a holy
man of God who is continually passing our way.
10 Let us make a small room on the roof with
walls and put there for him a bed, a table, a chair,
and a lamp so that whenever he comes to us, he can
go in there."*

*11 One day he came there, and he turned into the
chamber and rested there. 12 And he said to
Gehazi his servant, "Call this Shunammite."
When he had called her, she stood before him. 13*

> *And he said to him, "Say now to her, 'See, you have taken all this trouble for us; what is to be done for you? Would you have a word spoken on your behalf to the king or to the commander of the army?'" She answered, "I dwell among my own people." 14 And he said, "What then is to be done for her?" Gehazi answered, "Well, she has no son, and her husband is old." 15 He said, "Call her." And when he had called her, she stood in the doorway. 16 And he said, "At this season, about this time next year, you shall embrace a son." And she said, "No, my lord, O man of God; do not lie to your servant." 17 But the woman conceived, and she bore a son about that time the following spring, as Elisha had said to her.*

First, let me apologize in advance for the length of the scriptures. I have learned that I cannot assume that everyone knows these biblical accounts or remembers them in detail. The details mattered in ancient times and are equally vital for us today. Let me review quickly so we can jump into today's lesson on fierce faith. The first point worth mentioning is that:

1- **You cannot beat God giving.** The biblical text tells us that a wealthy, hospitable Shunammite Woman's concern for God's prophet set her up for unimaginable favor. Her hospitality escalated from ensuring he had a meal when he came through town to building a small room in her house for Elisha and his armor bearer. In modern times, this would be the equivalent of securing and relinquishing her "she-shed" or building a room over her garage. She provided shelter for them during their travels to her town. As a result, Elisha did some digging to find out how to bless her extraordinarily for her next-level accommodation.

2- **God will give you a blessing that you forgot you prayed.** I know that hit someone like a ton of bricks. All of us have those prayers almost entirely forgotten after we apply and adopt "finally faith" and release our private requests to God. If this were in modern times, maybe the Shunammite woman would show up to church late after all the children were checked into the children›s ministry. Perhaps she would take a long way home to avoid seeing the mothers playing in the park with their children. She may even get her groceries delivered to avoid seeing families shopping. Or she may have suppressed her desire so deeply that she pretended it didn›t bother her. Worse than that, maybe she experienced a little anxiety when she saw other mothers with their babies and dads with their kids, and she just shed a tear and wiped it away quickly. Somehow she had dealt with her deep longing, and as often as the prophet frequented her dwelling, he had no idea that having a child was her heart›s desire.

3- **Not only will God bless you, but He will do it when all the odds are stacked against you.** When Gehazi shared with Elisha how God could bless her, he noted that "her husband was old." That fact only made the miracle that much sweeter, as the prophet declared, "About this time next year, you will hold a son." And that manifest promise is exactly what occurred.

Now, you may be waiting to see the connection between a forgotten prayer and fierce faith. If so, do not fret; we are about to jump into it right now! Sometimes it takes more faith to hold onto your miracle than it does to get it, especially if it is a miracle you were not expecting in the first place.

Day 6 Scripture Part 2: 2 Kings 4:18-37

18 When the child had grown, he went out one day to his father among the reapers. 19 And he said to his father, "Oh, my head, my head!" The father said to his servant, "Carry him to his mother." 20 And when he had lifted him and brought him to his mother, the child sat on her lap till noon, and then he died. 21 And she went up and laid him on the bed of the man of God and shut the door behind him and went out. 22 Then she called to her husband and said, "Send me one of the servants and one of the donkeys, that I may quickly go to the man of God and come back again." 23 And he said, "Why will you go to him today? It is neither new moon nor Sabbath." She said, "All is well." 24 Then she saddled the donkey, and she said to her servant, "Urge the animal on; do not slacken the pace for me unless I tell you." 25 So she set out and came to the man of God at Mount Carmel.

When the man of God saw her coming, he said to Gehazi his servant, "Look, there is the

Shunammite. 26 Run at once to meet her and say to her, 'Is all well with you? Is all well with your husband? Is all well with the child?'" And she answered, "All is well." 27 And when she came to the mountain to the man of God, she caught hold of his feet. And Gehazi came to push her away. But the man of God said, "Leave her alone, for she is in bitter distress, and the Lord has hidden it from me and has not told me." 28 Then she said, "Did I ask my lord for a son? Did I not say, 'Do not deceive me?'" 29 He said to Gehazi, "Tie up your garment and take my staff in your hand and go. If you meet anyone, do not greet him, and if anyone greets you, do not reply. And lay my staff on the face of the child." 30 Then the mother of the child said, "As the Lord lives and as you yourself live, I will not leave you." So, he arose and followed her. 31 Gehazi went on ahead and laid the staff on the face of the child, but there was no sound or sign of life. Therefore, he returned to meet him and told him, "The child has not awakened."

Fierce Faith Plot Twist

Now, if this was a Netflix episode, and you were unfamiliar with this biblical account, you would be throwing popcorn at your screen right now! I know you would question the cruelty of a Creator that would give her the hidden, suppressed cry of her heart only to snatch the child away. Before you hit the "x" button and close out of the show to select another, let's recap the events.

The Shunammite was such a blessing to Elisha that he prayed for God to perform a miracle that only He could do. God grants Elisha's request and answers the woman's secret prayer. The woman gives birth to a healthy baby boy. She leaves him alone with his dad, and the son gets sick. The child's father panics and tells the servants to take their son to his mother. Before we get too upset with the dad, we need to recognize that some people don't know how to handle a crisis. Some people are unsure of what to do when a challenge arises. The best thing he could think of was to send the child to the person who had brought him into this world. His mother embraces and rocks him in her arms until his body grows limp and lifeless. At this moment, she activates a fierce

92

faith. This type of faith is an aggressive, insistent, resilient attitude that refuses to take *no* for an answer. This faith is a type of faith that proclaims, "It is not over until God says it is over." She tells her husband to bring her a servant and donkey so she can immediately get to the man of God. Again, her husband is confused and wondering why she is going. I love her response, "All will be well."

The next time somebody asks crazy questions at a time when you are trying to activate fierce faith, I want you to respond the way this faith-filled woman does. When someone attempts to slow you down while you are seeking God for a "suddenly" moment, I encourage you to respond similarly as the Shunammite woman does to her husband.

"It will all be well."

This blessed assurance is my modern-day answer when someone asks me the type of question her husband did. "Even if I am not okay right now, I will be." I have learned to answer like my grandmother, "All is well with my soul."

Sometimes you just don't have time to entertain questions because often, the questions are linked to the other person's lack of understanding or, worse, lack of faith. In your life's desperate and dire times, you must get to the people who can add their faith to yours and help you pull down strongholds and seize a breakthrough! The woman fell at the prophet's feet and basically was like, "Man of God, why in the world would you play my face? I know the Lord did not give me a baby to take him away. This situation must be fixed immediately!" That is the 21st-century *Book of Rainah* translation.

The Fierce Faith Circle is Small

The prophet heard her, felt her pain, and then gave her precise instructions. He told her not to speak to anyone and, if anyone talked to her, not to reply. This is super critical and reminds me of another story in the Bible that required fierce faith and the elimination of doubters from the room.

In Luke 8:49-56 NKJV, verse 29, expresses:

> *49 While He was still speaking, someone came from the ruler of the synagogue's house, saying to him, "Your daughter is dead. Do not trouble the Teacher."*

Jairus had finally made it to Jesus so He could heal his daughter and the servants came all the way to the revival just to tell Jairus that it was too late. Jesus ignored them and instructed Jairus to have fierce faith in verse 50: *But when Jesus heard it, He answered him, saying, "Do not be afraid; only believe, and she will be made well."*

Just know that there is always hope with the Lord on your side. Jesus encouraged the young girl's father and challenged him not to have fear but to have faith because faith is the key to unlocking the soon-to-come miracle. Jesus informs Jairus that if he believes, "she will be made well."

Notice that there was a part the father had to do: He had to believe before his miracle could become activated. In verses 51-55, we see an essential order that we need to replicate for fierce faith to produce the miracles we seek:

> *51 When He came into the house, He permitted no one to go in except Peter, James, and John, and the father and mother of the girl. 52 Now all wept and mourned for her; but He said, "Do not weep; she is not dead, but sleeping." 53 And they ridiculed Him, knowing that she was dead. 54 But He put them all outside, took her by the hand, and called, saying, "Little girl, arise." 55 Then her spirit returned, and she arose immediately. And He commanded that she be given something to eat.*

Now the next move of Jesus was crucial to the outcome. He took His ***Inner Circle*** in with Him and the other believers (the girls› parents). He put all the doubters **OUT!** Eventually, you will reach a point where you cannot hang out with the doubters. Because the doubters will cause you to waste your time. You will be mourning, weeping, and becoming depressed over a situation that God has allowed you to go through temporarily so that He might be glorified on Earth.

When you face bad news, and your challenge is looming, make sure you put "all" the doubters out—no matter who they are! I have experienced this necessity in my own life. For example, one of my daughters had "learning challenges" at school, and I was called to the school to meet with a team of specialists. This group of educators had been assembled to create an action plan for her educational process.

To my dismay, what I thought would be a meeting in which I was told she just needed to do a little work on reading turned into a one-and-half-hour deliberation. I was told everything "the experts" were going to "try," but they were pretty sure that she was going "fail" her grade because of how far behind she was. Thinking back, I remember asking them, "If she isn't learning, are you talking about putting her in a 'Special Needs' class?" They quickly informed me that they could not do that because she actually was the opposite of a "special needs" child. They reported that she was incredibly articulate, and her vocabulary was a couple of grades above her first-grade classmates. They continued to tell me that "she is behind, not because she can't learn, but because she either didn't learn or wasn't taught the information."

Now at this moment, I had a revelation. This situation would not end up the way any of the administrators expected. I decided right then and there that no matter what I had to do, my little girl would get caught up, and she would read on grade level. What is more, she was not going to be held back.

So, I started reaching out to friends and family members in the education field. I also reached out to friends who had children with similar issues, and I learned something in those next few hours. There are two types of people when you are facing a fiery trial (only two). First, there are believers, and second, there are doubters. After this revelation, I sprung into action. I succeeded in getting the educators in our lives on board. Then I reached out to all our family members who have a relationship with God. After that, we all started praying and working with her (because faith without works is dead). The results were incredible. First, our daughter went from being unable to read by the school system's standards to progressing to being on grade level by the end of the school year, but that is not the testimony. The testimony is that she continued to make more progress every single year. To the glory of God, the same child who practically could not read in the fall of her 1st-grade year went on to make a level 4 on her reading EOG in the 4th grade. The administrators were shocked, but I was not. I learned that God is able, and more importantly, I realized the necessity "to put the doubters out of the room" when there is a miracle on the line! Let's close out today with the season finale of the Shunammite woman's fierce faith on display.

Day 6 Scripture Part 1: 2 Kings 4:32-37

> *32 When Elisha came into the house, he saw the child lying dead on his bed. 33 So he went in and shut the door behind the two of them and prayed to the Lord. 34 Then he went up and lay on the child, putting his mouth on his mouth, his eyes on his eyes, and his hands on his hands. And as he stretched himself upon him, the flesh of the child became warm. 35 Then he got up again and walked once back and forth in the house and went up and stretched himself upon him. The child sneezed seven times, and the child opened his eyes.*

> *36 Then he summoned Gehazi and said, "Call this Shunammite." So, he called her. And when she came to him, he said, "Pick up your son." 37 She came and fell at his feet, bowing to the ground. Then she picked up her son and went out.*

The Specificity of God – The Details Matter

1- Atmosphere Matters

The boy's mother had placed him on the prophet's bed before she went to seek the prophet out. This seemingly small detail should not be overlooked. She lay the boy in a sacred space, a quiet place frequently inhabited by the man of God. The atmosphere, environment, and location are critical when you have activated fierce faith.

2- The methods may not be what you expect

It sounds as if Elisha gave the boy mouth-to-mouth resuscitation and prayed over him with specifics that only God could have given to the prophet.

3- The right faith leader makes a difference

The prophet went into the room alone. Do not estimate the power of godly men and women in your life. If your faith is weary, the fiercest thing you can do is to entrust the miracle with the faith leader you trust to help manifest your miracle.

4- God is *still* in the healing business

I want to encourage you to hold onto your fierce faith. God is the same yesterday, today, and tomorrow. He has been producing wonders since He separated day from night. And He is not through yet.

Fearless Faith To-Do List: Day 6

1. What prayer request has taken so long to come to pass that you had forgotten it until you read Day 6?

_____

_____

_____

_____

_____

_____

2. Please read the Fierce Faith Prayer below:

Dear Heavenly Father, We love you, and we thank You for loving us so much that You gave your only begotten Son as an atonement for our sins. We thank you that your timing is perfect and that you do all things well. We now approach you with open arms and open hearts as your children. We ask that the forgotten prayers of our hearts will manifest the same way you blessed the Shunammite woman so many centuries ago. Further, we request that by this time next season, you grant us the desire that we quietly set aside. And you would allow it to spring forth, exceedingly and abundantly above anything we could ask or think!

3. Record the date that God answers and exceeds your prayers: _____.

_____

_____

_____

_____

_____

_____

_____

_____

_____

_____

_____

_____

Day 7 Fervent Faith

fer·vent|
ˈfərvənt | adjective

having or displaying a passionate intensity:
showing great energy or enthusiasm in pursuit
of a cause or objective

> *Day 7 Scripture Part -1: James 5:16 (AMP)*
>
> *16 Therefore, confess your sins to one another [your false steps, your offenses], and pray for one another, that you may be healed and restored. The heartfelt and persistent prayer of a righteous man (believer) can accomplish much [when put into action and made effective by God—it is dynamic and can have tremendous power].*
>
> *Day 7 Scripture 2: Mark 7:24-30 (MSG)*
>
> *24-26 From there, Jesus set out for the vicinity of Tyre. He entered a house there where he didn't*

> *think he would be found, but he couldn't escape notice. He was barely inside when a woman who had a disturbed daughter heard where he was. She came and knelt at his feet, begging for help. The woman was Greek, Syro-Phoenician by birth. She asked him to cure her daughter.*
>
> *27 He said, "Stand in line and take your turn. The children get fed first. If there's any left over, the dogs get it."28 She said, "Of course, Master. But don't dogs under the table get scraps dropped by the children." 29-30 Jesus was impressed. "You're right! On your way! Your daughter is no longer disturbed. The demonic affliction is gone." She went home and found her daughter relaxed on the bed; the torment gone for good.*

I pray the Day 6 Devotion blessed you, it is one of the longer devotions in the book. Today's lesson is much shorter, but I pray that it is equally as powerful. There are four components needed for us to experience fervent faith.

1. Repentent Accoutability

First, fervent faith requires prayers for a restored, repentant, and righteous believer. The confession of your sins on the peer level activates this type of faith. I was taught that there are three levels of accountability, and I have expanded my faith to include a fourth. First, there is an **up** level. There are leaders, bosses, and authority figures who are **up** relationships. The next level encompasses **across** relationships; this level is often the most honest. This level contains your friends, siblings, cousins, co-workers, and classmates. The people on this level should be able to call you out and tell you, "Hey, you were wrong, sis. You need to get that right." They should be able to say, "Bro, you said those exact words? Yeah, we are going to see them right now to square this." Next, there is the **down** level. These are your children, mentees, and subordinates, anyone who looks up to you for leadership and guidance. I added internal accountability as the fourth level. No one knows you the same way you know yourself, so sometimes, you have to call bull crap on yourself and take action. Having multiple layers of accountability in your life helps you live more submitted to the biblical commandments.

When you have wise UP relationships, those people in this category help you because you are governed by their counsel, which can keep you out of trouble in the first place. We have already stated that your peers—the ACROSS crew, are the most important for two main reasons. First, because those are the people you typically are revealing your soul to; secondly, you confess your temptations to them. The DOWN relationships make you watch your actions because you know that someone is watching who can be impacted by the decisions you make and direction you take. The INNER relationship you have with yourself is critical because, to quote *De La Soul*, at the end of the day, it's just "Me, Myself, and I." I suggest you implement these levels of accountability if you don't already have them in your life.

2. Prayer + Faith In Action

It is not enough to be righteous. You repent and live justly before God to combine your prayers with your faith to access godly power on Earth. Our Heavenly Father has commanded us not only to have faith, like the saints found in the Roll Call of Faith in Hebrews 11. He has also required us to add faith to works because, without faith, it is impossible to please Him *(Hebrews 11:6)*. Also, faith without works is dead *(James 2:17)*.

3. Submitted, Aggressive Action

I love it when parents show up in the Bible because they seek miracles in a zealous, aggressive, borderline inappropriate way, yet that is a part of the blueprint for fervent faith. The Syrophoenician woman took a big chance approaching Jesus at all. Her status as a woman, gentile, and foreigner is noted in Mark 7:26. "Greek" is used to describe her. The description further designates her as a non-Jew (Bible Odyssey). All of these characteristics would make her "triply marginalized." *Bible Odyssey* also explains that "the children" are understood as the children of Israel or the Jews. This attribute is worth noting because, throughout scripture, Jesus expresses that His mission is primarily to reform the nation of Israel. "Dogs" (literally "little dogs") have a negative association in the Hebrew Bible (Ps 22:16) and in rabbinic literature, probably linked to the ferocious wild dogs in the Mediterranean world. In the New

Testament, they are also associated with impurity and otherness (Rev 22:15), so here, "dogs" means "outsiders" or non-Jews. This description by Jesus in Mark 7 is specifically linked to a period of Jesus's mission to the people of Israel, before the later expansion of the message to non-Jews."

In the Mark 7 account, this triply marginalized woman is in a predicament. Her daughter is suffering from demonic possession. For the sake of this story, let's say she was having a psychotic break and was afraid for her life. Let's step into our supernatural imagination and put ourselves in that mother's shoes. How would you respond if you had a child suffering from something that was terrorizing them, agonizing them, and you feared it might take their life? If you are like all the parents I know, you would approach the King of Kings and the Lord of Lords, and your pedigree would not matter one bit!

The Syrophoenician woman immediately fell at the feet of Jesus and stated her need. When Jesus denied her request, she was so persistent the disciples suggested that she be sent away. Jesus did not even address her directly.

Jesus replied by saying, *"I was not sent but unto the lost sheep of the house of Israel"* (Matthew 15:24). *"But she came and worshipped him, saying, Lord, help me"* (v. 25).

Not only did she not give up, but she also drew closer to Him and worshipped Him.

> *"And he said to her, Let the children first be filled: for it is not meet to take the children's bread and cast it to the dogs"* (Mark 7:27).

Biblical scholars note that after she worshipped Him, His tone softened, and He used the one word that gave her hope. He said, "let the children be filled first." That was the break she needed. She brilliantly expanded His parable and noted that even the dogs get the crumbs. She did not give up; she applied fervent faith to stay and stand firmly with Jesus until He acknowledged her request. There is one last thing this woman teaches us about fervent faith.

4. Refuse To Be Offended

I was an adult in my 30s before I read this scripture and realized that Jesus basically called this woman and her people "dogs." Yet, what surprised me more than what Jesus said was how the woman responded. She was so tapped into her fervent faith application to obtaining her daughter's healing that she didn't pop her neck, give Him a piece of her mind, or curse Him out. She just noted that even the dogs get the crumbs from the master's table!

I don't know who this is for, but in this season, you cannot afford to be offended. If you get laid off, shake the dust off your feet and go. If friends walk out of your life, wish them the best and love them from afar. If you don't get the promotion, keep doing your best work and know that better is coming. If your significant other breaks up with you or breaks your heart and you have to drop them like a hot potato, give them the gift of goodbye. Never forget that rejection is God's protection, direction, medication, and orchestration. God knows, and He cares; we just have to trust Him. In verses 29-30, we see that Jesus granted her request, and her daughter was not only cured; the Bible says that she was healed of the torment for good.

Fearless Faith To-Do List: Day 7

Read *Genesis 41: 50-52 (NIV):50 Before the years of famine came, two sons were born to Joseph by Asenath, daughter of Potiphera, priest of On. 51 Joseph named his firstborn Manasseh and said, "It is because God has made me forget all my trouble and all my father's household." 52 The second son he named Ephraim said, "It is because God has made me fruitful in the land of my suffering."*

#1 - Joseph is another great example of someone who also could have been offended but chose to apply fervent faith to his future. One of the sins you may need to confess to your peers is unforgiveness. After working in ministry for most of my adult life, I have found that even the most significant leaders and believers can struggle with this. First, if this is you, write down the name of an accountability partner that you can confess to and pray for forgiveness for the person who has offended you.

Accountability Partner: _____

_____

If you feel as if there is someone you have wronged, and it is appropriate to do so, you may need to approach them as the Bible instructs. Please note: the appropriateness of seeking out the wounded party depends significantly on the offense. If you need clarification, seek the counsel of an UP and ACROSS relationship before taking this step.

Offense Responsibility: _____
_____

#2 - List two areas where you can apply your faith boldly, like the Syrophoenician woman did in Mark, Chapter 7.

A. _____
_____
_____
_____
_____
_____
_____

B. _____

_____

_____

_____

_____

_____

_____

_____

_____

_____

_____

_____

_____

_____

_____

_____

Reference: https://www.bibleodyssey.org/en/people
/related-articles/syrophoenician-woman

FAITH FOUNDATION WEEK
RECAP & AFFIRMATION

I pray that this week blessed you and enriched your life. The goal was to help you face your fears and limiting beliefs. As we approach the next season of our lives, it will require us to overcome every doubt and lie of the enemy. Here is a Faith Foundation affirmation for you to memorize and recite:

> *You are enough.*
>
> *You are chosen.*
>
> *You are more than an overcomer.*
>
> *You shall live and not die.*
>
> *You are the lender and not the borrower.*
>
> *You will always have enough to give to someone else.*

Your faith is fully functional; it lacks nothing.

Your faith has an intentional inner circle of friends who are believers and not doubters.

Your faith is formulated and activated.

Your faith is fast-acting.

Your faith understands the power of "finally."

Your faith is fierce.

Your fervent, effectual faith prayers will avail much now and forever.

SCRIPTURE REFERENCES